Family Living™

CLASSICS

FAVORITE HOLIDAY COOKIES

Colorfully iced, sprinkled with cinnamon,
or chock-full of raisins or chocolate chips,
cookies are always a favorite Yuletide indulgence.

Colorful, delicious cookies for holiday parties & gifts
Iced Cookies • Brownies • Biscotti • Gingerbread • Refrigerator Dough

Leisure Arts, Inc.
Little Rock, Arkansas
www.leisurearts.com

HONEY ORNAMENT COOKIES

Be inspired by vintage striped ornaments to "paint" these Honey Ornament Cookies with colorful icings.

COOKIES
- 1/2 cup butter or margarine, softened
- 1/3 cup vegetable shortening
- 1 cup sugar
- 1/4 cup honey
- 1 egg
- 1/2 teaspoon vanilla extract
- 3 cups all-purpose flour
- 1/4 teaspoon salt

ICING
- 6 2/3 cups sifted confectioners sugar
- 6 to 7 tablespoons water
- 1 tablespoon light corn syrup
- 1 teaspoon vanilla extract
- Red, green, yellow, and blue paste food coloring

Preheat oven to 350 degrees. Trace ornament patterns, on this page, onto stencil plastic; cut out. For cookies, cream butter, shortening, and sugar in a large bowl until fluffy. Add honey, egg, and vanilla; beat until smooth. In a medium bowl, combine flour and salt. Add dry ingredients to creamed mixture; stir until a soft dough forms. Divide dough in half. On a lightly floured surface, use a floured rolling pin to roll out half of dough to 1/8-inch thickness. Use patterns and a sharp knife to cut out cookies. If dough is sticky, frequently dip knife into flour while cutting out cookies. Transfer cookies to a greased baking sheet. Use a plastic drinking straw to cut a hole in top of each cookie. Bake 5 to 7 minutes or until bottoms are lightly browned. Transfer cookies to a wire rack to cool.

For icing, combine confectioners sugar, water, corn syrup, and vanilla in a medium bowl; stir until smooth. Divide icing into 5 small bowls. Tint red, green, yellow, blue; leave remaining icing white. Spoon icing into pastry bag fitted with small round tips. Pipe outline of each color of designs onto cookies; fill in with icing. Let icing harden. Store in single layer in an airtight container.
Yield: about 5 dozen cookies

...ed to resemble lollipops, Sugarplum Cookies are divine confections.

UGARPLUM COOKIES

- 4 cups sifted confectioners sugar
- ½ to 4 tablespoons water
- 1 tablespoon light corn syrup
- 1 teaspoon vanilla extract
  Green and red paste food coloring
- 1 package (11 ounces) firm sugar cookies (about 2 inches in diameter)

In a medium bowl, combine ...nfectioners sugar, water, corn syrup, and vanilla; beat until smooth. Transfer about ½ cup icing into each of 3 small bowls. Tint green and red, leaving remaining icing white. Spoon each icing into a pastry bag fitted with a small round tip. Working with 3 cookies at a time, outline and fill in tops of cookies with a thin layer of green or red icing. While icing is still wet, pipe white icing onto cookies in a spiral design. Place on a wire rack to let icing harden. Store in an airtight container.

Yield: about 2 dozen cookies

Shown on back cover: The proof is in the pudding—these cookies are chock-full of flavor! We used three pudding mixes and a variety of flavored chips to create a trio of yummy Pudding Cookies.

PUDDING COOKIES

We made 3 separate cookie recipes for 3 different flavors.

- 1 cup butter or margarine, softened
- 1/2 cup granulated sugar
- 1/2 cup firmly packed brown sugar
- 2 eggs
- 2 teaspoons vanilla extract
- 2 1/2 cups all-purpose flour
- 1 teaspoon baking soda
- 1/4 teaspoon salt

Preheat oven to 350 degrees. In a large bowl, cream butter and sugars until fluffy. Add eggs and vanilla; beat until smooth. In a medium bowl, combine flour, baking soda, salt, and ingredients from one of the variations. Add dry ingredients to creamed mixture; stir until a soft dough forms. Drop by tablespoonfuls onto a lightly greased baking sheet. Bake 9 to 11 minutes or until bottoms are lightly browned. Transfer cookies to a wire rack to cool. Store in an airtight container.
Yield: about 4 dozen cookies

VARIATIONS
CHOCOLATE: 3.9-ounce package chocolate instant pudding mix and 6-ounce package semisweet chocolate chips

BUTTERSCOTCH: 3.4-ounce package butterscotch instant pudding mix and 7 1/2-ounce package almond brickle chips

LEMON: 3.4-ounce package lemon instant pudding mix and 10-ounce package semisweet chocolate chips

LEMON SANDWICH COOKIES

- 1 1/2 packages (12 ounces each) butter-flavored crackers
- 1 can (16 ounces) lemon-flavored ready-to-spread frosting
- 2 pounds, 10 ounces vanilla-flavored candy coating
- 1/4 teaspoon lemon-flavored oil (used in candy making)

Place half of crackers (about 75 crackers) on waxed paper. Spoon frosting into a pastry bag fitted with a large round tip. Pipe about 1 teaspoon frosting onto each cracker. Place remaining crackers on top of frosting and press lightly. In a heavy medium saucepan, melt candy coating and lemon oil over low heat. Remove from heat. Place each cracker sandwich on a fork and dip into candy coating until covered. Place on waxed paper and allow candy coating to harden. Store in an airtight container in a cool place.
Yield: about 6 dozen sandwich cookies

CINNAMON COOKIES

Shown on page 6.

COOKIES

- 1¹/₂ cups vegetable shortening
- 3¹/₂ cups sugar
- 2 eggs
- ¹/₂ cup water
- 1 teaspoon vanilla extract
- 5 cups all-purpose flour
- 1 tablespoon ground cinnamon
- 2 teaspoons baking powder
- 1 teaspoon salt

ICING

- ³/₄ cup vegetable shortening
- 4¹/₄ cups confectioners sugar
- 1 teaspoon vanilla extract
- 4 to 5 tablespoons milk

Preheat oven to 375 degrees. For cookies, cream shortening and sugar in a large bowl until fluffy. Add eggs, water, and vanilla; beat until smooth. In a large bowl, combine flour, cinnamon, baking powder, and salt. Add dry ingredients to creamed mixture; stir until a soft dough forms. Shape dough into 1-inch balls and place 2 inches apart on a greased baking sheet; flatten balls into 2-inch-diameter cookies with bottom of a glass dipped in sugar. Bake 7 to 9 minutes or until bottoms are lightly browned. Transfer cookies to a wire rack to cool.

For icing, combine shortening, confectioners sugar, vanilla, and milk in a large bowl; beat until smooth. Spoon icing into a pastry bag fitted with a small star tip. Refer to photo on page 6 and pipe a snowflake design onto each cookie. Let icing harden. Store in an airtight container.

Yield: about 9 dozen cookies

BUTTERSCOTCH COOKIES

Shown on page 6.

- ¹/₂ cup butter or margarine, softened
- ¹/₃ cup granulated sugar
- ¹/₃ cup firmly packed brown sugar
- 1 egg
- 1 teaspoon vanilla extract
- 1 cup butterscotch chips, melted
- 2¹/₃ cups all-purpose flour
- ³/₄ teaspoon baking soda
  Purchased red decorating icing
  Green candy-coated chocolate pieces

Preheat oven to 375 degrees. In a large bowl, cream butter and sugars until fluffy. Add egg and vanilla, beating until smooth. Stir in melted butterscotch chips. In a medium bowl, combine flour and baking soda. Stir dry ingredients into creamed mixture. On a lightly floured surface, use a floured rolling pin to roll out dough to ¹/₄-inch thickness. Use a doughnut cutter to cut out cookies. Transfer to a greased baking sheet. Bake 8 to 10 minutes or until brown. Cool completely on a wire rack. Using a leaf tip and icing, refer to photo on page 6 to pipe a bow onto each cookie. Press a candy-coated piece on each bow before icing hardens. Let icing harden. Store in an airtight container.
Yield: about 2¹/₂ dozen 3-inch cookies

Share the flavor of Christmas with a batch of snowflake-frosted Cinnamon Cookies (recipe on page 5)

Cut in a wreath shape, crispy Butterscotch Cookies (recipe on page 5) are embellished with red icing bows and green candies.

6

a sweet surprise, hang these Round Ornament Cookies on a little tree. Made with ingredients u probably already have in the cupboard, the cookies are cut from a simple pattern and iced in ght colors. You'll want to have extra cookies for nibbling, too. The recipe is on page 8.

ROUND ORNAMENT COOKIES

Shown on page 7.

COOKIES
- 1/2 cup butter or margarine, softened
- 1/3 cup vegetable shortening
- 1/2 cup granulated sugar
- 1/2 cup firmly packed brown sugar
- 1/4 cup dark corn syrup
- 1 egg
- 1 teaspoon vanilla extract
- 3 cups all-purpose flour
- 1/4 teaspoon salt

ICING
- 6 2/3 cups confectioners sugar
- 1/2 cup water
- 1 tablespoon light corn syrup
- 1 teaspoon vanilla extract
  Red, green, yellow, and blue paste food coloring

Trace ornament pattern, page 9, onto stencil plastic; cut out. Preheat oven to 350 degrees. For cookies, cream butter, shortening, and sugars in a large bowl until fluffy. Add corn syrup, egg, and vanilla; beat until smooth. In a medium bowl, combine flour and salt. Add dry ingredients to creamed mixture; stir until a soft dough forms. Divide dough in half. On a lightly floured surface, use a floured rolling pin to roll out half of dough to 1/8-inch thickness. Use pattern and a sharp knife to cut out cookies. Transfer to a greased baking sheet. Use a plastic drinking straw to cut a hole in top of each cookie. Bake 6 to 8 minutes or until bottoms are lightly browned. Transfer cookies to a wire rack to cool. Repeat with remaining dough.

For icing, combine confectioners sugar, water, corn syrup, and vanilla in a medium bowl; stir until smooth. Place 1/4 cup white icing in a small bowl and cover. Divide remaining icing into 4 small bowls; tint icing red, green, yellow, and blue. Spoon icing into pastry bags fitted with small round tips. Use tinted icing to pipe outline around edges of cookies; fill in with icing. Let icing harden. Use white icing to pipe highlight onto each cookie. Store in a single layer in an airtight container.
Yield: about 4 1/2 dozen cookies

BANANA-NUT COOKIES

These cookies freeze well.

- 2 packages (7.6 ounces each) banana-nut muffin mix
- 1 cup quick-cooking oats
- 1/4 teaspoon ground cinnamon
- 2 eggs
- 1/4 cup vegetable oil
- 2 tablespoons milk

Preheat oven to 350 degrees. In a medium bowl, combine muffin mix, oats, and cinnamon. In a small bowl, beat eggs, oil, and milk until blended. Add to dry ingredients; stir until a soft dough forms. Drop tablespoonfuls of dough onto an ungreased baking sheet. Bake 10 to 12 minutes or until bottoms are lightly browned. Transfer cookies to a wire rack to cool. Store in an airtight container.
Yield: about 3 dozen cookies

Light and delicate, Snowflake Meringue Cookies (recipe on page 10) are a lovely treat for cookie lovers. The confections are flavored with almond and cinnamon and piped into a snowflake pattern using a pastry bag fitted with a small star tip.

SNOWFLAKE MERINGUE COOKIES

Shown on page 9.

    4   egg whites
1 1/2   cups sifted confectioners sugar
    1   teaspoon almond extract
  1/2   teaspoon ground cinnamon
  1/2   teaspoon cream of tartar
        White crystal sugar

Trace pattern, on page 9, onto tracing paper. Cover greased baking sheets with waxed paper.

In a large bowl, beat egg whites until foamy. Add confectioners sugar, almond extract, cinnamon, and cream of tartar; beat until very stiff. Spoon meringue into a pastry bag fitted with a small star tip. For each cookie, place pattern under waxed paper and use as a guide to pipe meringue onto waxed paper. Sprinkle with crystal sugar. Allow cookies to sit at room temperature 30 minutes.

Preheat oven to 200 degrees. Bake 2 hours. Leaving cookies on waxed paper, remove waxed paper from baking sheet while cookies are still warm; cool completely. Carefully peel away waxed paper. Store in an airtight container.
Yield: about 2 1/2 dozen cookies

SNOWBALL COOKIES

Shown on page 16.

    2   cups sifted confectioners sugar
    6   cups crisp rice cereal
    1   cup raisins
    1   cup chopped pecans
    4   cups miniature marshmallows
  1/4   cup butter or margarine
    1   teaspoon vanilla extract
  1/2   teaspoon almond extract

Place confectioners sugar in a large bowl. In another large bowl, combine cereal, raisins, and pecans.

In a medium saucepan, combine marshmallows and butter. Stirring constantly, cook over medium heat until smooth. Remove from heat; stir in extracts. Pour marshmallow mixture over cereal mixture; stir until well coated. Using greased hands, shape mixture into 1 1/2-inch balls. Coat with sugar. Store in an airtight container.
Yield: about 6 1/2 dozen cookies

CRANBERRY CHRISTMAS COOKIES

- 1 cup fresh cranberries
- $1/2$ cup vegetable shortening
- $1^1/2$ cups sugar
- 1 egg
- 2 tablespoons buttermilk
- 1 teaspoon vanilla extract
- $1/4$ teaspoon orange extract
- 2 cups all-purpose flour
- $1/2$ teaspoon baking soda
- $1/2$ teaspoon ground cinnamon
- $1/2$ teaspoon ground cloves
- $1/2$ teaspoon ground nutmeg
- $1/4$ teaspoon salt
- 1 cup chopped walnuts
- 1 cup golden raisins

Preheat oven to 375 degrees. Process cranberries in a food processor until coarsely ground. In a large bowl, cream shortening and sugar until fluffy. Add egg, buttermilk, and extracts; beat until smooth. Stir in cranberries. In a small bowl, combine flour, baking soda, cinnamon, cloves, nutmeg, and salt. Add dry ingredients to creamed mixture; stir until a soft dough forms. Stir in walnuts and raisins. Drop teaspoonfuls of dough onto a greased baking sheet. Bake 9 to 11 minutes or until bottoms are lightly browned. Transfer cookies to a wire rack to cool. Store in an airtight container.

Yield: about 7 dozen cookies

PEPPERMINT SWIRL COOKIES

- 1 package (18 ounces) refrigerated sugar cookie dough
- $1/4$ cup finely crushed peppermint candies (about 10 round candies)
- $1/8$ teaspoon red liquid food coloring

Divide sugar cookie dough in half. On a sheet of plastic wrap, use a floured rolling pin to roll out half of dough into an 8-inch square. Knead peppermint candies and food coloring into remaining half of dough. On a separate sheet of plastic wrap, roll out peppermint dough into an 8-inch square. Place peppermint dough on top of plain dough. Using plastic wrap, roll dough into an 8-inch-long roll. Wrap in plastic wrap and store in refrigerator.

Yield: 1 roll cookie dough

To bake: Cut dough into $1/4$-inch slices. Place 2 inches apart on a lightly greased baking sheet. Bake 8 to 10 minutes in a 350-degree oven. Cool cookies on baking sheet 5 minutes; transfer to a wire rack to cool completely. Store in an airtight container.

Yield: about $2^1/2$ dozen cookies

COUNTRY CHRISTMAS TREES

COOKIES
- 1/2 cup butter or margarine, softened
- 1/2 cup firmly packed brown sugar
- 1/2 cup molasses
- 1 egg
- 1 teaspoon vanilla extract
- 2 1/2 cups all-purpose flour
- 1 teaspoon ground ginger
- 1 teaspoon ground cinnamon
- 1/4 teaspoon ground nutmeg
- 1/4 teaspoon ground cloves
- 1/4 teaspoon salt
- Craft sticks

ICING
- 1 1/2 cups sifted confectioners sugar
- 3 tablespoons vegetable shortening
- 2 to 3 teaspoons milk
- 1 teaspoon vanilla extract
- Red, yellow, and green paste food coloring

For cookies, trace tree pattern, on this page, onto stencil plastic; cut out. In a large bowl, cream butter and brown sugar until fluffy. Add molasses, egg, and vanilla; beat until smooth. In a medium bowl, combine flour, ginger, cinnamon, nutmeg, cloves, and salt. Add dry ingredients to creamed mixture; stir until a soft dough forms. Divide dough in half. Wrap in plastic wrap and chill 2 hours.

Preheat oven to 350 degrees. On a lightly floured surface, use a floured rolling pin to roll out half of dough to 1/4-inch thickness. Use pattern and a sharp knife to cut out cookies. Transfer to a greased baking sheet. Push a craft stick into bottom of each cookie. Bake 8 to 10 minutes or until edges are lightly browned. Cool cookies on baking sheet 2 minutes; transfer to a wire rack to cool completely. Repeat with remaining dough.

For icing, beat confectioners sugar, shortening, milk, and vanilla in a small bowl until smooth. Place 1/4 cup icing in each of 2 small bowls; tint icing red and yellow. Tint remaining icing green. Transfer icing to pastry bags fitted with small round tips. Refer to photo on page 13 to outline trees with green icing. Pipe small and large red or yellow dots on each tree. Let icing harden. Store in a single layer in an airtight container.
Yield: about 1 1/2 dozen cookies

MAPLE-NUT MACAROONS

- 3 egg whites
- 1/2 teaspoon cream of tartar
- 3/4 cup plus 2 tablespoons sugar
- 2 cups chopped pecans, toasted and finely ground
- 2 tablespoons maple syrup
- 1 teaspoon vanilla extract

Preheat oven to 300 degrees. In a medium bowl, beat egg whites and cream of tartar until foamy. Gradually add sugar, beating until stiff peaks form. Fold in pecans, maple syrup, and vanilla. Drop by rounded teaspoonfuls onto a baking sheet lined with parchment paper. Bake 15 to 18 minutes or until bottoms are lightly browned. Transfer cookies to a wire rack to cool. Store in a airtight container.
Yield: about 6 dozen cookies

st for fun, these Country Christmas Tree cookies are baked on sticks and "rooted" in excelsior-filled
ay pots. Brightly colored icing trims the trees with holiday flair.

PEANUT BUTTER CRUMB COOKIES

1 cup butter or margarine, softened
1 cup extra-crunchy peanut butter
3/4 cup firmly packed brown sugar
3/4 cup granulated sugar
2 eggs
1 1/2 teaspoons vanilla extract
2 1/2 cups all-purpose flour
1 teaspoon baking powder
1 teaspoon baking soda
1/2 teaspoon salt
1 1/2 cups coarsely crushed cinnamon graham crackers (about 22 squares), divided
1/2 cup finely chopped dry-roasted peanuts

Preheat oven to 350 degrees. In a large bowl, cream butter, peanut butter, and sugars until fluffy. Add eggs and vanilla; beat until smooth. In a medium bowl, combine flour, baking powder, baking soda, and salt. Add dry ingredients to creamed mixture; beat until well blended. Stir in 1 cup cracker crumbs. In a small bowl, combine peanuts and remaining 1/2 cup cracker crumbs. Roll heaping teaspoonfuls of dough into balls; roll in crumb mixture. Place balls on a lightly greased baking sheet; flatten with a fork. Bake 7 to 9 minutes or until lightly browned. Transfer to a wire rack to cool. Store in an airtight container.
Yield: about 7 dozen cookies

TOFFEE ALMOND COOKIES

1 cup butter or margarine, softened
2 cups firmly packed brown sugar
2 eggs
1 teaspoon almond extract
1 teaspoon vanilla extract
3 cups all-purpose flour
1 teaspoon baking powder
1/2 teaspoon salt
1 package (7 1/2 ounces) almond brickle chips
1 cup slivered almonds, toasted

Preheat oven to 350 degrees. In a large bowl, cream butter and brown sugar until fluffy. Add eggs and extracts; beat until smooth. In a medium bowl, combine flour, baking powder, and salt. Add dry ingredients to creamed mixture; beat until well blended. Stir in brickle chips and almonds. Drop by heaping teaspoonfuls onto a greased baking sheet. Bake 8 to 10 minutes or until bottoms are lightly browned. Transfer cookies to a wire rack to cool. Store in an airtight container.
Yield: about 7 dozen cookies

ORANGE SLICE COOKIES

COOKIES

- 1 cup butter or margarine, softened
- 1 cup granulated sugar
- $1/2$ cup confectioners sugar
- 1 egg
- 1 teaspoon orange extract
- $1/4$ teaspoon orange paste food coloring
- $2^1/2$ cups all-purpose flour
- $1/2$ teaspoon baking powder
- $1/4$ teaspoon salt

ICING

- $3/4$ cup confectioners sugar
- 1 tablespoon butter or margarine
- 1 tablespoon vegetable shortening
- $1/4$ teaspoon vanilla extract
- $1/8$ teaspoon orange extract
- 1 to 2 teaspoons milk

Preheat oven to 375 degrees. For cookies, cream butter and sugars in a large bowl until fluffy. Add egg, orange extract, and food coloring; beat until smooth. In a medium bowl, combine flour, baking powder, and salt. Add dry ingredients to creamed mixture; stir until soft dough forms. On a lightly floured surface, use a floured rolling pin to roll out dough to $1/4$-inch thickness. Use a -inch-diameter round cookie cutter to cut out cookies. Cut each cookie in half. Place cookies 2 inches apart on greased baking sheet. Using a table knife, make indentations in cookies to resemble orange segments. Bake 7 to minutes or until bottoms are lightly browned. Transfer cookies to a wire rack to cool.

For icing, combine confectioners sugar, butter, shortening, extracts, and milk in a small bowl; beat until smooth. Transfer icing to a pastry bag fitted with small round tip. Pipe outline onto each cookie. Let icing harden. Store in an airtight container.
Yield: about 5 dozen cookies

EASY COCONUT MACAROONS

- 2 cups all-purpose baking mix
- 1 can (14 ounces) sweetened condensed milk
- 1 egg
- 1 teaspoon vanilla extract
- 1 can ($3^1/2$ ounces) flaked coconut Vegetable cooking spray
- 2 tablespoons sugar
- 5 ounces red candied cherries, halved

Preheat oven to 350 degrees. In a large bowl, combine baking mix, sweetened condensed milk, egg, and vanilla; beat until well blended. Stir in coconut. Drop teaspoonfuls of dough onto a cookie sheet sprayed with cooking spray. Sprinkle tops of cookies with sugar. Bake 6 to 8 minutes or until bottoms are golden brown. Press a cherry half into center of each warm cookie. Transfer cookies to a wire rack to cool. Store in an airtight container.
Yield: about 6 dozen cookies

Sure to bring smiles to children's faces, Jolly Snowman Cookies are cleverly decorated with pretzels and chocolate chips. Snowball Cookies (recipe on page 10) made with crisp rice cereal, raisins, pecans, and marshmallows are sure to become a favorite sweet treat.

JOLLY SNOWMAN COOKIES

  1   cup butter or margarine, softened
1¹/₂ cups granulated sugar
  1   egg
  1   teaspoon vanilla extract
2³/₄ cups all-purpose flour
 ¹/₄ teaspoon salt
      Pretzels
      Miniature chocolate chips

Preheat oven to 350 degrees. In a medium bowl, cream butter and sugar until fluffy. Add egg and vanilla; beat until smooth. In a small bowl, combine flour and salt. Add dry ingredients to creamed mixture; stir until a soft dough forms. For each cookie, shape 3 small balls of dough, graduated in size. Place on a greased baking sheet and flatten balls slightly to resemble a snowman (cookies should be about 4¹/₂-inches long). Break pretzels into twig shapes. Insert pieces of broken pretzels into sides of cookies for arms. Press small pieces of pretzels onto cookies for mouths. Press chocolate chips onto cookies for eyes, noses, and buttons. Bake 10 to 12 minutes or until edges are light brown. Cool completely on a wire rack. Store in an airtight container.
Yield: about 14 cookies

Beautifully decorated with icing and food coloring, each Santa Cookie is a little work of art. The buttery cookies, shaped in a cookie mold, are richly spiced with coriander.

SANTA COOKIES

COOKIES

1	cup butter or margarine, softened
1	cup firmly packed brown sugar
1/2	cup granulated sugar
1	egg
1	teaspoon vanilla extract
3 1/2	cups all-purpose flour
1	teaspoon ground coriander
1/4	teaspoon salt

ICING

6	tablespoons sifted confectioners sugar
4	teaspoons milk
	Burgundy, green, and black paste food coloring

Preheat oven to 350 degrees. For cookies, cream butter and sugars in a medium bowl until fluffy. Add egg and vanilla; beat until smooth. In a small bowl, combine flour, coriander, and salt.

Add dry ingredients to creamed mixture; stir until a soft dough forms. Press small pieces of dough into a greased and lightly floured cookie mold. Use a sharp knife to loosen edges of dough. Invert mold onto a greased baking sheet. Tap edge of mold lightly to release dough. Repeat for remaining dough. Bake 10 to 12 minutes or until edges of cookies are brown. Transfer to a wire rack to cool completely.

For icing, combine sugar and milk until smooth. To decorate cookies, dilute food coloring with a small amount of water. Referring to photo, use a paintbrush to paint food coloring on each cookie. Use a clean paintbrush to brush white icing on cookie for beard, mustache, eyebrows, and trim on coat, hat, and sled. Brush icing lightly over each sled. Allow icing to harden. Store in an airtight container.

Yield: about 1 dozen 5-inch cookies

17

CHOCOLATE-PEANUT BUTTER COOKIES

This cookie dough can be made ahead and frozen.

- 1/2 cup butter or margarine, softened
- 1/2 cup crunchy peanut butter
- 1/2 cup firmly packed brown sugar
- 1/2 cup granulated sugar
- 1 egg
- 1 teaspoon vanilla extract
- 1 2/3 cups all-purpose flour
- 1/2 teaspoon baking powder
- 1/4 teaspoon salt
- 1 cup semisweet chocolate mini chips

In a large bowl, cream butter, peanut butter, and sugars until fluffy. Add egg and vanilla; beat until smooth. In a small bowl, combine flour, baking powder, and salt. Add dry ingredients to creamed mixture; stir until a soft dough forms. Stir in chocolate chips. Divide dough into thirds. Shape each third into a 7-inch-long roll. Wrap in plastic wrap and refrigerate until well chilled or store in freezer.

If frozen, let dough thaw at room temperature 15 minutes. Preheat oven to 375 degrees. With a serrated knife, cut dough into 1/4-inch slices. Place on an ungreased baking sheet. Bake 7 to 9 minutes or until bottoms are golden brown. Transfer to a wire rack to cool. Store in an airtight container.

Yield: about 6 dozen cookies, or 2 dozen cookies per roll

QUICK GINGERBREAD COOKIES

- 1 package (1 pound, 2 ounces) refrigerated sugar cookie dough
- 2 teaspoons molasses
- 1/4 to 1/2 cup all-purpose flour, divided
- 1 tablespoon ground cinnamon
- 1/8 teaspoon ground ginger
- 1 to 2 teaspoons cocoa (optional)

Preheat oven to 350 degrees. Flatten dough on a lightly floured surface. Drizzle molasses over dough. Sprinkle 1/4 cup flour, cinnamon, and ginger over dough. For a darker dough, add cocoa with dry ingredients. Knead ingredients into dough until well blended, using additional flour as necessary. On a lightly floured surface, use a floured rolling pin to roll out dough to 1/4-inch thickness. Use a cookie cutter to cut out dough (we used a 3 1/2 x 4-inch bear-shaped cutter). Transfer to a greased baking sheet. Bake 6 to 8 minutes or until bottoms are lightly browned. Transfer cookies to a wire rack to cool. Store in an airtight container.

Yield: about 1 dozen cookies

CHERRY BIT COOKIES

1¼ cups butter or margarine, softened
2¼ cups sugar
2 eggs
1½ teaspoons vanilla extract
1 teaspoon cherry flavoring
4½ cups all-purpose flour
1 teaspoon baking powder
¾ teaspoon salt
1 jar (10 ounces) maraschino cherries, finely chopped and well drained

In a large bowl, cream butter and sugar until fluffy. Add eggs, vanilla, and cherry flavoring; beat until smooth. In a medium bowl, combine flour, baking powder, and salt. Add dry ingredients to creamed mixture; stir until a soft dough forms. Stir in cherries. Divide dough into fourths and wrap in plastic wrap; chill 2 hours.

Preheat oven to 350 degrees. On a lightly floured surface, use a floured rolling pin to roll out one fourth of dough to ⅛-inch thickness. Use a 4-inch-wide heart-shaped cookie cutter to cut out cookies. Transfer to an ungreased baking sheet. Bake 8 to 10 minutes or until bottoms are lightly browned. Transfer cookies to a wire rack to cool. Repeat with remaining dough. Store in an airtight container.

Yield: about 3½ dozen cookies

SLICE-AND-BAKE COOKIES

¾ cup butter or margarine, softened
1¼ cups sugar
1 egg
1 teaspoon vanilla extract
2 cups all-purpose flour
½ teaspoon salt

In a large bowl, cream butter and sugar until fluffy. Add egg and vanilla; beat until smooth. In a small bowl, combine flour and salt. Add dry ingredients to creamed mixture; stir until a soft dough forms. Divide dough in half. Place each half on plastic wrap. Use plastic wrap to shape dough into two 8-inch-long rolls. Chill 3 hours or until firm (if rolls have flattened, reshape into a round shape).

Preheat oven to 375 degrees. Cut dough into ¼-inch slices. Place 1 inch apart on a lightly greased baking sheet. Bake 6 to 8 minutes or until bottoms are lightly browned. Transfer cookies to a wire rack to cool. Store in an airtight container.

Yield: about 5 dozen cookies or 2½ dozen cookies per roll

Baked to crispy perfection, these simple, melt-in-your-mouth Star Cookies are a stellar holiday idea.

STAR COOKIES

- ³/₄ cup butter or margarine, softened
- ¹/₂ cup sugar
- 1 egg
- 1 teaspoon vanilla extract
- 1³/₄ cups all-purpose flour
- 3 tablespoons cornstarch
- ¹/₂ teaspoon baking powder
- ¹/₈ teaspoon salt

Preheat oven to 350 degrees. In a medium bowl, cream butter and sugar until fluffy. Add egg and vanilla; beat until smooth. In a small bowl, combine flour, cornstarch, baking powder, and salt. Add dry ingredients to creamed mixture; stir until a soft dough forms. On a lightly floured surface, use a floured rolling pin to roll out dough to ¹/₈-inch thickness. Use a 2³/₄-inch-wide scalloped-edge star-shaped cookie cutter to cut out cookies. Transfer to a greased baking sheet. Bake 7 to 9 minutes or until bottoms are lightly browned. Transfer cookies to a wire rack to cool. Store in an airtight container. **Yield:** about 4 dozen cookies

Windows made of melted hard candy highlight your choice of cookie cutter shapes in these Christmas Card Cookies.

CHRISTMAS CARD COOKIES

- 1 cup butter or margarine, softened
- 1 cup granulated sugar
- 2 eggs
- 1 teaspoon vanilla extract
- 3 1/3 cups all-purpose flour
- 1 teaspoon baking powder
- 1/2 teaspoon salt
  Vegetable cooking spray
- 2 cups hard candies (we used 40 candies each of red and green)
  Red and green paste food coloring and ribbon to decorate

In a large bowl, cream butter and sugar until fluffy. Add eggs and vanilla; beat until smooth. In a medium bowl, combine flour, baking powder, and salt. Add dry ingredients to creamed mixture; stir until a soft dough forms. Cover and refrigerate 1 hour.

Preheat oven to 350 degrees. Line baking sheets with aluminum foil; spray foil with cooking spray. On a lightly floured surface, use a floured rolling pin to roll out dough to 1/4-inch thickness. Using a sharp knife, cut dough into 4 x 5-inch rectangles. Transfer cookies to prepared baking sheets, leaving 1 inch between cookies. Using desired cookie

Continued on page 22

Continued from page 21

cutters or patterns, cut out shapes from center of each rectangle. For each cookie, use a drinking straw to make 2 holes $1/2$ inch apart at top or one side edge for ribbon. Bake 12 to 14 minutes or until cookies are firm. Cool completely on foil.

In separate small saucepans, melt each color of hard candy over medium heat. Spoon desired color of melted candy into each cutout shape in cookies. Allow candy to harden. If desired, use a small paintbrush to paint details on cookies with food coloring. Carefully remove cookies from foil. Thread ribbon through holes in cookies and tie as desired. Store in an airtight container.
Yield: about $1^1/2$ dozen cookies

COFFEE LACE COOKIES

- 1 cup finely chopped pecans
- 2 tablespoons instant coffee granules
- 2 tablespoons hot water
- $1/2$ cup butter, softened
- $1/2$ cup firmly packed brown sugar
- 2 tablespoons whipping cream
- $1/4$ cup all-purpose flour
- $1/4$ teaspoon salt
- $1/8$ teaspoon baking soda
- 1 cup quick-cooking rolled oats
- 12 ounces semisweet baking chocolate, chopped

Preheat oven to 350 degrees. To toast pecans, spread evenly on an ungreased baking sheet and bake 5 to 8 minutes, stirring once. Cool completely on pan.

In a small bowl, dissolve coffee granules in water. In a large bowl, cream butter and sugar until fluffy. Beat in coffee mixture. In a small saucepan, heat cream over medium heat until boiling. Reduce heat to medium-low and simmer 2 to 3 minutes. Add cream to coffee mixture and stir until well blended. In a small bowl, combine flour, salt, and baking soda. Stir dry ingredients into creamed mixture. Stir in oats and pecans. Drop heaping teaspoonfuls of batter 4 inches apart onto a greased baking sheet. Use fingers to press each cookie into a 2-inch circle. Bake 8 minutes (cookies will be soft); cool on pan 3 minutes. Transfer to a wire rack to cool completely.

Stirring constantly, melt chocolate over low heat in a small saucepan. Spread chocolate over bottom of each cookie. Return to wire rack, chocolate side up. Allow chocolate to harden. Store in an airtight container in a cool dry place.
Yield: about $3^1/2$ dozen cookies

CINNAMON FINGERS

Shown on page 25.

- 1/2 cup granulated sugar
- 1/2 teaspoon ground cinnamon
- 1 cup butter, softened
- 1/2 cup firmly packed brown sugar
- 1 teaspoon vanilla extract
- 2 cups all-purpose flour
- 1 cup finely ground pecans
- 1/4 teaspoon salt

Preheat oven to 350 degrees. In a small bowl, combine granulated sugar and cinnamon; set aside.

In a medium bowl, cream butter, brown sugar, and vanilla until fluffy. Stir in flour, pecans, and salt. Shape dough into 3-inch-long rolls. Place each roll in sugar mixture and spoon sugar mixture over until well coated. Place on a greased baking sheet. Bake 15 to 18 minutes or until light brown. Transfer to a wire rack to cool completely. Store in an airtight container.

Yield: about 4 1/2 dozen cookies

MACADAMIA SHORTBREADS

Shown on page 24.

- 2 cups all-purpose flour
- 2 jars (7 ounces each) whole macadamia nuts, divided
- 1/4 teaspoon salt
- 1 cup butter, softened
- 1/2 cup firmly packed brown sugar
- 1 teaspoon vanilla extract

Preheat oven to 350 degrees. In a blender or food processor, process flour, 1 cup macadamia nuts, and salt until finely ground. In a medium bowl, cream next 3 ingredients until fluffy. Stir in flour mixture. Shape into 1-inch balls and place 2 inches apart on a greased baking sheet. Press 1 macadamia nut into center of each cookie. Bake 12 to 15 minutes or until edges are light brown. Cool completely on a wire rack.

Yield: about 5 dozen cookies

CASHEW CRESCENTS

Shown on page 24.

- 3/4 cup butter, softened
- 1/2 cup granulated sugar
- 1 egg yolk
- 1 1/2 cups all-purpose flour
- 1 cup finely chopped dry-roasted cashews
  Sifted confectioners sugar

Preheat oven to 350 degrees. In a medium bowl, cream butter and sugar until fluffy. Add egg yolk; stir until smooth. Add flour and cashews; stir until a soft dough forms. Shape tablespoonfuls of dough into crescent shapes and place 1 inch apart on a greased baking sheet. Bake 12 to 15 minutes or until edges are light brown. While cookies are still warm, coat with confectioners sugar. Transfer to a wire rack to cool completely. Coat with confectioners sugar again. Store in an airtight container.

Yield: about 3 dozen cookies

Have a very merry cookie swap! An old-fashioned cookie swap is a tasty way to share Christmas spirit with friends. Everyone brings along a batch or two of their favorite cookies—enough for each guest to take some home after plenty of munching.

Clockwise from top left: These cookies are sure to become favorites: Cashew Crescents (recipe on page 23), Chocolate Crisp Cookies (page 26), Wafer Roll Cookies (page 26), Cinnamon Fingers (page 23), Crunchy Pecan Cookies (page 27), Raspberry Fudgies (page 44), Chocolate-Orange Balls (page 34), Sesame Cookies (page 27), Pecan-Caramel Brownies (page 45), and Macadamia Shortbreads (page 23).

25

WAFER ROLL COOKIES

Shown on page 24.

- 1/2 cup butter or margarine, softened
- 1/2 cup granulated sugar
- 1/2 cup all-purpose flour
- 2 egg whites
- 1 teaspoon vanilla extract
- 3 ounces semisweet baking chocolate, chopped
- 1/2 cup finely chopped pecans

Preheat oven to 400 degrees. In a medium bowl, cream butter and sugar until fluffy. Stir in flour. In a small bowl, beat egg whites until foamy. Beat egg whites and vanilla into creamed mixture. Drop teaspoonfuls of dough 4 inches apart onto a heavily greased baking sheet; flatten slightly. Bake 5 to 6 minutes or until edges are light brown. While cookies are still warm, roll each cookie around the end of a wooden spoon. Transfer to a wire rack, seam side down, to cool completely.

Stirring constantly, melt chocolate over low heat in a small saucepan. Dip ends of each cookie in chocolate and then in pecans. Return to wire rack; allow chocolate to harden. Store in an airtight container.

Yield: about 3 dozen cookies

CHOCOLATE CRISP COOKIES

Shown on page 24.

- 3 cups (one 12-ounce and one 6-ounce package) semisweet chocolate chips, divided
- 1/2 cup butter or margarine, softened
- 1 1/2 cups granulated sugar
- 4 eggs
- 1 tablespoon vanilla extract
- 1/2 teaspoon chocolate extract
- 1 cup sifted all-purpose flour
- 1 teaspoon baking powder
- 1/4 teaspoon salt

Preheat oven to 350 degrees. Stirring constantly, melt 1 cup chocolate chips over low heat in a small saucepan. Remove from heat. In a medium bowl, cream butter and sugar until fluffy. Add melted chocolate chips, eggs, and extracts; beat until smooth. In a small bowl, combine flour, baking powder, and salt. Add dry ingredients to creamed mixture; stir until a soft dough forms. Stir in remaining 2 cups chocolate chips. Drop tablespoonfuls of dough 2 inches apart onto a greased baking sheet. Bake 15 to 17 minutes or until cookies are cracked on top. Immediately place on a wire rack to cool completely. Allow baking sheet to cool completely between batches. Store in an airtight container.

Yield: about 5 dozen cookies

CRUNCHY PECAN COOKIES

Shown on page 25.

- 1 cup butter or margarine, softened
- 1 cup granulated sugar
- 1 cup firmly packed brown sugar
- 1 cup vegetable oil
- 1 egg
- 1 teaspoon vanilla extract
- 3 1/2 cups all-purpose flour
- 1 teaspoon baking soda
- 1/2 teaspoon salt
- 2 cups finely crushed corn flake cereal
- 1 1/2 cups chopped pecans

Preheat oven to 350 degrees. In a large bowl, cream butter and sugars until fluffy. Beat in oil, egg, and vanilla. In a medium bowl, combine flour, baking soda, and salt. Add dry ingredients to creamed mixture; stir until a soft dough forms. Stir in cereal crumbs and pecans. Drop tablespoonfuls of dough 2 inches apart onto a greased baking sheet. Using a fork dipped in water, make a crisscross design on each cookie. Bake 10 to 12 minutes or until edges are light brown. Transfer to a wire rack to cool completely. Store in an airtight container.
Yield: about 7 dozen cookies

SESAME COOKIES

Shown on page 25.

- 1 cup all-purpose flour
- 1/2 cup sifted confectioners sugar
- 1/2 cup cornstarch
- 1 cup butter, softened
- 1/4 cup sesame seeds, toasted

In a medium bowl, combine flour, sugar, and cornstarch. Using a pastry blender or 2 knives, cut butter into dry ingredients until mixture resembles coarse meal. Knead on a lightly floured surface until a soft dough forms. Shape into a 12-inch-long roll. Coat with sesame seeds. Wrap in plastic wrap and refrigerate 1 hour.

Preheat oven to 300 degrees. Cut dough into 1/4-inch-thick slices and place on a greased baking sheet. Bake 20 to 25 minutes or until edges are light brown. Cool completely on a wire rack.
Yield: about 3 1/2 dozen cookies

EASY FRUITCAKE COOKIES

Shown on page 28.

- 1 package (1 pound, 2 ounces) refrigerated sugar cookie dough
- 1/4 cup all-purpose flour
- 1/2 teaspoon ground allspice
- 1 container (4 ounces) red candied cherries, chopped
- 1 container (4 ounces) green candied cherries, chopped
- 1/2 cup chopped walnuts

Let dough sit at room temperature 15 minutes. Preheat oven to 350 degrees. In a small bowl, combine flour and allspice. Break up dough in a large bowl. Sprinkle flour mixture over dough; stir until flour is incorporated. Stir in cherries and walnuts. Drop teaspoonfuls of dough 2 inches apart onto a greased baking sheet. Bake 9 to 11 minutes or until edges are lightly browned. Transfer cookies to a wire rack to cool. Store in an airtight container.
Yield: about 4 1/2 dozen cookies

Fruitcake has been a Christmas tradition for generations. Now it's even easier to carry on the custom with our Easy Fruitcake Cookies. Using refrigerated cookie dough, the chewy treats can be made in a snap (recipe on page 27).

*stive shapes and the tempting aroma of cinnamon make our Spicy Christmas Tree Cookies a treat
*at the entire family can enjoy (recipe on page 30).

SPICY CHRISTMAS TREE COOKIES

Shown on page 29.

COOKIES

- $^2/_3$ cup firmly packed brown sugar
- $^2/_3$ cup molasses
- $^3/_4$ cup butter or margarine
- 1 egg
- 1 teaspoon orange extract
- $3^1/_2$ cups all-purpose flour
- 2 teaspoons ground cinnamon
- $^1/_2$ teaspoon ground cardamom
- $^1/_2$ teaspoon baking soda

ICING

- $1^1/_2$ cups sifted confectioners sugar
- 1 to 2 tablespoons water
- $^1/_2$ teaspoon vanilla extract
- $^1/_4$ to $^1/_2$ teaspoon red paste food coloring

For cookies, combine brown sugar and molasses in a heavy small saucepan. Stirring constantly, cook over medium-high heat until mixture boils. Boil 1 minute; remove from heat. In a large bowl, combine butter and hot sugar mixture; stir until butter melts. Add egg and orange extract; beat until well blended. In a medium bowl, combine flour, cinnamon, cardamom, and baking soda. Add dry ingredients to butter mixture; stir until well blended. Divide dough into thirds. Wrap in plastic wrap and chill 2 hours.

Preheat oven to 350 degrees. On a lightly floured surface, use a floured rolling pin to roll out one third of dough into a 9-inch-high x 14-inch-wide rectangle. Make 3-inch-wide lengthwise cuts with a knife. Use a scalloped-edged pastry cutter to make a diagonal cut from upper left corner to $4^1/_8$ inches from lower left corner (Fig. 1).

Fig. 1

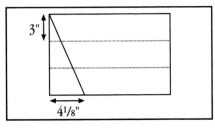

Make a second diagonal cut $2^3/_4$ inches from first cut (Fig. 2).

Fig. 2

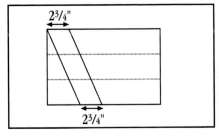

Continue making diagonal cuts $2^3/_4$ inches from previous cuts. Refer to Fig. 3 to make a diagonal cut $2^3/_4$ inches from upper left corner to lower lengthwise cut.

Fig. 3

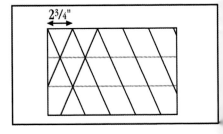

Continue to make diagonal cuts $2^3/_4$ inches from previous cut to form triangles. Transfer to a lightly greased baking sheet. Bake 5 to 7 minutes or until edges are lightly browned. Transfe cookies to a wire rack to cool. Repeat with remaining dough.

For icing, combine confectioners sugar, water, and vanilla in a small bowl; stir until smooth. Tint red. Spoon icing into a pastry bag fitted with a small round tip. Pipe design onto cookies. Allow icing to harden. Store in an airtight container.

Yield: about 6$^1/_2$ dozen cookies

GERMAN CHOCOLATE COOKIES

1   package (18.25 ounces) German chocolate cake mix with pudding mix
1   container (8 ounces) vanilla-flavored yogurt
1   egg
1   can (about 15 ounces) coconut-pecan ready-to-spread frosting

Preheat oven to 350 degrees. In a large bowl, combine cake mix, yogurt, and egg; beat until smooth. Drop teaspoonfuls of dough 2 inches apart onto a greased baking sheet. Bake 10 to 12 minutes or until bottoms are lightly browned. Transfer cookies to a wire rack; ice warm cookies. Store in a single layer in an airtight container.

Yield: about 6 dozen cookies

CHOCOLATE-ORANGE-SPICE COOKIE MIX

8   cups all-purpose flour
2$^1/_2$ cups granulated sugar
2$^1/_2$ cups firmly packed brown sugar
1   cup cocoa
1   tablespoon dried orange peel
2   teaspoons ground cinnamon
2   teaspoons ground ginger
1$^1/_2$ teaspoons baking soda
1   teaspoon salt
2$^3/_4$ cups chilled butter or margarine, cut into pieces

In a very large bowl, combine flour, sugars, cocoa, orange peel, cinnamon, ginger, baking soda, and salt. Using a pastry blender or 2 knives, cut in butter until mixture resembles coarse meal. Divide mix evenly into 4 resealable plastic bags (about 4$^1/_2$ to 5 cups mix per bag). Store in refrigerator.

Yield: about 18 cups cookie mix

To bake: Bring one bag of cookie mix to room temperature before mixing. Preheat oven to 375 degrees. In a medium bowl, combine cookie mix, 1 egg, 2 tablespoons milk, and 2 teaspoons vanilla extract; beat with an electric mixer until a soft dough forms. Divide dough in half. On a heavily floured surface, use a floured rolling pin to roll out half of dough to slightly less than $^1/_8$-inch thickness. Use desired cookie cutter to cut out cookies. Transfer to a lightly greased baking sheet. Bake 4 to 6 minutes or until bottoms are lightly browned. Transfer cookies to a wire rack to cool. Repeat with remaining dough. Store in an airtight container.

Yield: about 5 dozen cookies (when we used a 4-inch-wide by 3$^1/_2$-inch-high reindeer-shaped cookie cutter)

EASY PUDDING COOKIES

- 1 cup buttermilk baking mix
- 1 package (3.4 ounces) instant chocolate pudding and pie filling mix
- 1/3 cup vegetable oil
- 1 egg, beaten
- 1/4 cup English toffee bits
- 2 tablespoons sugar

Preheat oven to 350 degrees. In a large bowl, combine baking mix, pudding mix, oil, and egg; stir until a soft dough forms. Stir in toffee bits. Drop teaspoonfuls of dough 2 inches apart onto a greased baking sheet. Flatten with the bottom of a glass dipped in sugar. Bake 5 to 7 minutes or until edges are lightly browned. Transfer cookies to a wire rack to cool. Store in an airtight container.
Yield: about 3 1/2 dozen cookies

CHOCOLATE-KISSED COOKIES

- 1 package (20 ounces) refrigerated sugar cookie dough
- 1 package (14 ounces) milk chocolate candies with almonds

Preheat oven to 350 degrees. Drop 1 teaspoon cookie dough into each cup of an ungreased miniature muffin pan. Press chocolate candies into dough. Bake 8 minutes or until edges are lightly browned. Cool cookies in pan 5 minutes; transfer to a wire rack to cool completely. Store in an airtight container.
Yield: about 5 dozen cookies

CHRISTMAS BUTTON COOKIES

- 1 cup butter or margarine, softened
- 1 package (3 ounces) cream cheese, softened
- 1 cup sugar
- 1 egg yolk
- 1 teaspoon almond extract
- 2 1/2 cups all-purpose flour
- 1 package (4 ounces) red candied cherries
- 1 package (4 ounces) green candied cherries

In a large bowl, cream butter, cream cheese, and sugar until fluffy. Add egg yolk and almond extract; beat until smooth. Add flour to creamed mixture; stir until a soft dough forms. Wrap in plastic wrap and chill 1 hour.
Preheat oven to 325 degrees. Shape dough into 1-inch balls and place 2 inches apart on a greased baking sheet. Use thumb to make a slight indentation in top of each ball. Bake 12 to 15 minutes or until bottoms of cookies are lightly browned. Press a candied cherry into indentation in each warm cookie. Transfer cookies to a wire rack to cool. Store in an airtight container.
Yield: about 5 1/2 dozen cookies

Sweeter than a smooch under the mistletoe, Chocolate-Kissed Cookies are so easy to make. Just drop spoonfuls of refrigerated cookie dough in miniature muffin tins and press a chocolate candy into each piece.

Button, button, who's got the button? We have lots of them, and they taste delightful! Christmas Button Cookies are a cute way to make the merry Yuletide days even brighter.

CHOCOLATE-ORANGE BALLS

Shown on page 25.

    1 package (12 ounces) semisweet
         chocolate chips
 1 1/2 cups vanilla wafer crumbs
    3/4 cup sifted confectioners sugar
    1/2 cup sour cream
    2 teaspoons dried grated orange
         peel
    1/4 teaspoon salt
   10 pieces orange slice gumdrop
         candy, cut into quarters
         Sifted confectioners sugar

Stirring constantly, melt chocolate chips in a large saucepan over low heat. Remove from heat; stir in cookie crumbs, sugar, sour cream, orange peel, and salt. Cover and chill until firm. Press crumb mixture around each piece of candy, forming 1 1/2-inch balls. Coat with confectioners sugar. Store in an airtight container.
Yield: 40 balls

ORANGE-NUT SNOWBALLS

    1 cup butter or margarine, softened
    2 cups confectioners sugar, divided
    1 teaspoon grated orange zest
    1 teaspoon orange extract
    1/2 teaspoon vanilla extract
 2 1/4 cups all-purpose flour
    1/4 teaspoon salt
    1 cup chopped walnuts, toasted and
         coarsely ground

Preheat oven to 350 degrees. In a large bowl, cream butter and 1/2 cup confectioners sugar until fluffy. Stir in orange zest and extracts. In a medium bowl, combine flour and salt. Add dry ingredients to creamed mixture; stir until a soft dough forms. Stir in walnuts. Shape dough into 1-inch balls and place 2 inches apart on an ungreased baking sheet. Bake 12 to 15 minutes or until bottoms are lightly browned. Roll warm cookies in remaining 1 1/2 cups confectioners sugar. Place cookies on waxed paper; cool completely. Roll in confectioners sugar again. Store in an airtight container.
Yield: about 4 dozen cookies

LEMON-NUT BALLS

    1 package (16 ounces)
         confectioners sugar
    1 package (12 ounces) vanilla
         wafers, finely crushed
    1 cup chopped pecans, toasted and
         finely ground
    1/2 cup butter or margarine, melted
    1 can (6 ounces) frozen lemonade
         concentrate, thawed
    1/2 teaspoon lemon extract
         Confectioners sugar and
         flaked coconut

In a large bowl, combine confectioners sugar, vanilla wafers, and pecans. In a small bowl, combine melted butter, lemonade concentrate, and lemon extract; add to confectioner sugar mixture, stirring until well combined. Shape mixture into 1-inch balls. Roll half of balls in confectioners sugar and remaining balls in coconut. Store in an airtight container in refrigerator.
Yield: about 7 dozen balls

CHOCOLATE-COCONUT BARS

Shown on page 36.

 1 package (18¼ ounces) chocolate cake mix with pudding in the mix
 ⅓ cup unsalted butter or margarine, softened
 1 egg
 1½ cups flaked coconut
 1 cup slivered almonds, toasted and coarsely chopped
 ¾ cup semisweet chocolate mini chips
 ½ cup firmly packed brown sugar
 ½ cup granulated sugar
 1 egg
 ¼ cup cream of coconut
 2 tablespoons all-purpose flour
 1 teaspoon vanilla extract

Preheat oven to 325 degrees. Line a 9 x 13-inch baking pan with aluminum foil, extending foil over ends of pan; grease foil. In a medium bowl, combine cake mix, butter, and 1 egg; beat until well blended (mixture will be crumbly). Firmly press mixture into bottom of prepared pan. Sprinkle coconut, almonds, and chocolate chips over crust. In a medium bowl, combine sugars and egg; beat until smooth. Add cream of coconut, flour, and vanilla; beat just until blended. Spread mixture into pan. Bake 28 to 32 minutes or until set and lightly browned. Cool in pan on a wire rack. Use ends of foil to lift from pan. Cut into 2-inch squares. Store in an airtight container in a cool place.
Yield: about 2 dozen bars

FRUIT MUESLI BARS

 1 package (18.25 ounces) yellow cake mix
 ½ cup firmly packed brown sugar
 ¾ cup butter or margarine, softened
 1½ cups strawberry muesli cereal
 1 jar (12 ounces) strawberry preserves

Preheat oven to 350 degrees. Combine cake mix and brown sugar in a large bowl; use a pastry blender to cut in butter. Stir in cereal. Reserve 1½ cups of mixture. Press remaining cereal mixture into an ungreased 9 x 13-inch baking pan. Spread preserves over crust almost to edges of pan. Sprinkle remaining cereal mixture over preserves. Bake 35 to 38 minutes or until top is lightly browned. Cool in pan on a wire rack. Cut into 1 x 2-inch bars. Store in an airtight container.
Yield: about 4 dozen bars

These moist Chocolate-Coconut Bars (recipe on page 35) give you a head start on preparation with a packaged cake mix.

spice-cake crust complements the flavor of creamy Pumpkin Spice Bars (recipe on page 38).
ey're easy to make using a cake mix and canned pumpkin.

PUMPKIN SPICE BARS

Shown on page 37.

- 1 package (18.25 ounces) spice cake mix
- 1 egg
- 2 tablespoons butter or margarine, melted
- 1 package (8 ounces) cream cheese, softened
- 1 can (14 ounces) sweetened condensed milk
- 1 can (16 ounces) pumpkin
- 2 eggs
- $1/2$ teaspoon salt
- 1 cup chopped pecans

Preheat oven to 350 degrees. In a large bowl, combine cake mix, 1 egg, and melted butter; stir until mixture is well blended (mixture will be dry). Press into bottoms of three 8 x 5 x 1-inch aluminum foil pans or one $10^1/2$ x $15^1/2$-inch jellyroll pan. In another large bowl, beat cream cheese until fluffy. Add sweetened condensed milk, pumpkin, 2 eggs, and salt; beat until mixture is smooth. Pour over crust. Sprinkle pecans over filling. Bake 30 to 35 minutes or until filling is set. Cool in pan on a wire rack 20 minutes; chill. Cut into $1^1/2$-inch bars. Store in an airtight container in refrigerator.
Yield: about 5 dozen bars

CRUNCHY FUDGE BARS

- 1 package ($22^1/2$ ounces) fudge brownie mix and ingredients to prepare brownies
- 1 cup coarsely chopped salted peanuts
- 2 packages (3 ounces each) cream cheese, softened
- $1/4$ cup crunchy peanut butter
- 1 egg
- 1 package (16 ounces) chocolate-flavored confectioners sugar
- $3/4$ cup almond brickle chips

Preheat oven to 350 degrees. Line a $10^1/2$ x $15^1/2$-inch jellyroll pan with aluminum foil, extending foil over ends of pan; grease foil. Prepare brownie batter according to package directions. Stir in peanuts. Spread batter into prepared pan. In a medium bowl, beat cream cheese and peanut butter until fluffy. Add egg; beat until smooth. Gradually add confectioners sugar and beat until smooth. Spread over batter. Sprinkle with brickle chips. Bake 30 to 34 minutes or until center is almost set. Cool in pan.

Use ends of foil to lift brownies from pan. Cut into 2-inch squares. Store in an airtight container.
Yield: about 3 dozen brownies

NORTH POLE GRANOLA BARS

- 1/4 cup butter or margarine, softened
- 3/4 cup firmly packed brown sugar
- 1/2 cup crunchy peanut butter
- 1/4 cup light corn syrup
- 1 egg
- 1 teaspoon vanilla extract
- 3/4 cup all-purpose flour
- 1/2 teaspoon baking powder
- 1 1/2 cups quick-cooking oats
- 2 packages (6 ounces each) chopped dried fruit
- 1/2 cup chopped salted peanuts

Preheat oven to 325 degrees. Line a x 13-inch baking pan with aluminum oil, extending foil over ends of pan. ghtly grease foil. In a medium bowl, eam butter and brown sugar until uffy. Add peanut butter, corn syrup, gg, and vanilla; beat until smooth. In a nall bowl, combine flour and baking owder. Add dry ingredients to creamed ixture; stir until a soft dough forms. ir in oats, fruit, and peanuts. Press ixture into prepared pan. Bake 30 33 minutes or until firm and lightly owned. Cool in pan. Use ends of foil lift from pan. Cut into 2 x 4-inch bars. rap individually or store in an airtight ntainer.
eld: about 1 dozen bars

CHOCOLATE-COCONUT SHORTBREAD WEDGES

- 1 1/2 cups flaked coconut
- 1 1/2 cups slivered almonds, toasted
- 1 cup butter, softened
- 2/3 cup sugar
- 1 1/2 teaspoons vanilla extract
- 1 2/3 cups all-purpose flour
- 1/3 cup cocoa
- 1/2 teaspoon salt

Preheat oven to 350 degrees. Process coconut and almonds in a food processor until coarsely ground. In a medium bowl, cream butter and sugar until fluffy. Beat in vanilla. In a small bowl, combine flour, cocoa, and salt. Gradually add dry ingredients; beat just until blended. Stir in coconut mixture. Divide dough into thirds. Pat each third of dough into a 7-inch-diameter circle on a baking sheet lined with parchment paper. Bake 25 to 30 minutes or until firm. Transfer baking sheet to a wire rack; cool 10 minutes. Transfer shortbread on paper to a firm surface. Cut each warm shortbread into 8 wedges; cool completely. Store in an airtight container.
Yield: 2 dozen shortbread wedges

S'MORE CHOCOLATE BARS

1 package (21.1 ounces) brownie mix
$1/2$ cup vegetable oil
$1/2$ cup water
1 egg
7 graham crackers ($2^1/_2$ x 5-inch rectangles), coarsely crumbled
$1^1/_2$ cups semisweet chocolate chips
3 cups miniature marshmallows

Preheat oven to 350 degrees. In a large bowl, combine brownie mix, oil, water, and egg; stir until well blended. Pour into a greased 9 x 13-inch baking pan. Sprinkle cracker crumbs over batter. Bake 20 minutes. Sprinkle chocolate chips over brownies; top with marshmallows. Bake 8 to 10 minutes longer or until marshmallows begin to brown. Cool in pan on a wire rack. Use an oiled knife to cut into 1 x 2-inch bars. Store in an airtight container.
Yield: about 4 dozen bars

PEANUTTY S'MORE BARS

6 graham crackers ($2^1/_2$ x 5-inch rectangles)
2 jars (7 ounces each) marshmallow creme
$2/_3$ cup plus 1 tablespoon crunchy peanut butter, divided
1 package (6 ounces) semisweet chocolate chips

Coarsely crumble crackers into a lightly greased 9 x 13-inch baking pan. Stirring frequently, melt marshmallow creme and $2/_3$ cup peanut butter in a medium saucepan over medium-low heat. Immediately pour marshmallow mixture over cracker pieces, spreading with a spatula if necessary. Stirring frequently, melt chocolate chips and remaining 1 tablespoon peanut butter i a small saucepan over low heat. Drizzle over marshmallow mixture. Chill 2 hour or until firm. Cut into 1 x 2-inch bars. Store in an airtight container in a single layer in refrigerator.
Yield: about 4 dozen bars

ORANGE-WALNUT BARS

CRUST

- 1 package (18$\frac{1}{4}$ ounces) orange cake mix
- $\frac{1}{3}$ cup vegetable oil
- $\frac{1}{3}$ cup applesauce
- 1 egg
- 1 teaspoon vanilla extract
- $\frac{2}{3}$ cup flaked coconut

TOPPING

- 1 cup sugar
- $\frac{1}{3}$ cup butter or margarine
- $\frac{1}{3}$ cup milk
- 1 cup white baking chips
- 1 cup chopped walnuts

Preheat oven to 350 degrees. Line a 9 x 13-inch baking pan with waxed paper; grease waxed paper. For crust, combine cake mix, oil, applesauce, egg, vanilla, and coconut in a medium bowl; beat until well blended. Spread mixture into prepared pan. Bake 20 to 25 minutes or until edges are lightly browned. While crust is baking, prepare topping.

For topping, combine sugar, butter, and milk in a heavy medium saucepan over medium-high heat. Stirring constantly, bring mixture to a boil and boil 1 minute. Reduce heat to low. Add baking chips; stir until smooth. Stir in walnuts. Spread hot topping over warm crust. Cool in pan. Cut into 1 x 2-inch bars. Store in an airtight container.

Yield: about 4 dozen bars

CHOCOLATE-AMARETTO BISCOTTI

Shown on page 42.

This biscotti keeps well for several days.

- $\frac{1}{2}$ cup butter or margarine, softened
- 1 cup sugar
- 2 eggs
- 3 tablespoons amaretto
- $\frac{1}{2}$ teaspoon almond extract
- 2$\frac{1}{4}$ cups all-purpose flour
- $\frac{1}{4}$ cup cocoa
- 1 teaspoon baking powder
- $\frac{1}{2}$ teaspoon baking soda
- $\frac{1}{4}$ teaspoon salt
- 1 cup sliced almonds, toasted

Preheat oven to 375 degrees. Grease and flour a baking sheet. In a large bowl, cream butter and sugar until fluffy. Add eggs, amaretto, and almond extract; beat until smooth. In a medium bowl, combine flour, cocoa, baking powder, baking soda, and salt. Add dry ingredients to creamed mixture; stir until a soft dough forms. Stir in almonds. Divide dough into thirds. Allow 3 inches between loaves on prepared baking sheet. Shape each piece of dough into a 2 x 9-inch loaf, flouring hands as necessary. Bake 20 to 24 minutes or until loaves are firm. Cool 10 minutes on baking sheet.

Cut loaves diagonally into $\frac{1}{2}$-inch slices. Lay slices flat on an ungreased baking sheet. Bake 6 minutes; turn slices over and bake 6 minutes longer. Transfer cookies to a wire rack to cool. Store in a cookie tin.

Yield: about 4 dozen cookies

To create cookies with a gourmet twist, bake Chocolate-Amaretto Biscotti (recipe on page 41). These crispy toast-like confections have a delicate flavor and a serious crunch, and they're wonderful for dipping in coffee or cocoa.

r a treat that's as easy to fix as it is good to eat, try these Chocolate-Peanut Butter Cups. Using a
ckage of refrigerated peanut butter cookie dough makes this recipe super quick.

HOCOLATE-PEANUT UTTER CUPS

1 package (18 ounces) refrigerated peanut butter cookie dough
1 bag (13 ounces) mini peanut butter cups

Preheat oven to 350 degrees. Shape dough into 1-inch balls. Place balls in greased cups of a miniature muffin pan. Press peanut butter cups into center of each ball. Bake 10 to 12 minutes or until edges are firm. Cool in pan 5 minutes. Remove from pan and cool completely on a wire rack. Store in an airtight container.

Yield: about 3 dozen cookies

RASPBERRY FUDGIES

Shown on page 25.

CRUST
- 1/2 cup butter or margarine
- 2 ounces unsweetened baking chocolate, chopped
- 1 cup granulated sugar
- 2 eggs
- 1/8 teaspoon raspberry-flavored oil (used in candy making)
- 1/2 cup all-purpose flour
- 1/2 cup chopped pecans
- 1 tablespoon vanilla extract

TOPPING
- 1/4 cup raspberry jelly
- 1 cup granulated sugar
- 1/3 cup evaporated milk
- 2 tablespoons butter or margarine
- 1/2 cup semisweet chocolate chips
- 1/4 cup marshmallow creme
- 1 tablespoon vanilla extract
- 1 cup chopped pecans

Preheat oven to 350 degrees. For crust, melt butter and chocolate over low heat in a small saucepan, stirring constantly. Remove from heat. In a medium bowl, beat sugar and eggs until foamy. Gradually add chocolate mixture and raspberry-flavored oil; beat until smooth. Stir in flour, pecans, and vanilla. Spoon batter into a greased 9 x 13-inch baking dish. Bake 25 to 30 minutes or until set in center.

For topping, spread jelly evenly over warm crust; cool completely. In a medium saucepan, combine sugar, milk and butter. Stirring occasionally, bring to a boil over medium heat. Stirring constantly, boil 5 minutes. Remove from heat. Add chocolate chips, marshmallow creme, and vanilla; stir until smooth. Stir in pecans. Immediately pour topping over jelly. Cool completely in pan. Cut into 1-inch squares. Store in an airtight container.

Yield: about 8 dozen fudgies

CHOCOLATE BROWNIES

- 1/2 cup butter or margarine, softened
- 1 cup granulated sugar
- 4 eggs
- 1 1/2 cups chocolate-flavored syrup
- 1 teaspoon vanilla extract
- 18 chocolate wafer cookies, finely ground
- 1/2 cup all-purpose flour
- 1 package (6 ounces) semisweet chocolate chips

Preheat oven to 350 degrees. In a medium bowl, cream butter and sugar until fluffy. Beat in next 3 ingredients. Add cookie crumbs and flour; mix until well blended. Stir in chocolate chips. Pour into a greased and floured 9 x 13-inch baking pan. Bake 40 to 45 minutes or until dry on top and set in center. Cool in pan. Cut into squares. Store in an airtight container.

Yield: about 1 1/2 dozen brownies

PUMPKIN BROWNIES

BROWNIES

- 3/4 cup butter or margarine, softened
- 3/4 cup firmly packed brown sugar
- 3/4 cup granulated sugar
- 1 teaspoon vanilla extract
- 1 cup canned pumpkin
- 2 eggs
- 1/2 cups all-purpose flour
- 1/2 cup cocoa
- 2 teaspoons baking powder
- 3/4 teaspoon pumpkin pie spice
- 1/4 teaspoon salt

ICING

- 4 cups confectioners sugar
- 1/3 cup cocoa
- 1/3 cup butter or margarine, softened
- 1/4 cup boiling water
- 1 teaspoon vanilla extract

Preheat oven to 350 degrees. For brownies, cream butter, sugars, and vanilla in a large bowl until fluffy. Beat pumpkin and eggs until smooth. In a small bowl, combine flour, cocoa, baking powder, pumpkin pie spice, and salt. Gradually add dry ingredients to creamed mixture; beat until well blended. Spread batter into a greased 10 1/2 x 15 1/2-inch jellyroll pan. Bake 14 to 16 minutes or until a toothpick inserted in center of brownies comes out with a few crumbs clinging to it. Cool in pan on a wire rack.

For icing, combine confectioners sugar and cocoa in a medium bowl. Add butter, water, and vanilla; beat until smooth. Spread icing on brownies. Cut into 2-inch squares. Store in an airtight container.

Yield: about 3 dozen brownies

PECAN-CARAMEL BROWNIES

Shown on page 24.

- 1 box (21 1/2 ounces) brownie mix
- 1/2 cup water
- 1/4 cup vegetable oil
- 1 egg
- 1 bag (14 ounces) caramel candies
- 2 tablespoons milk
- 1 package (6 ounces) semisweet chocolate chips
- 1 cup chopped pecans, divided

Preheat oven to 350 degrees. In a medium bowl, combine brownie mix, water, oil, and egg; mix just until moistened. Spread one half of batter in a greased 9 x 13-inch baking pan. Bake 10 minutes.

In a small saucepan, combine caramels and milk. Stirring occasionally, cook over medium heat until smooth. Remove from heat. Sprinkle chocolate chips and 1/2 cup pecans over partially baked batter. Drizzle caramel mixture over pecans. Spread remaining batter over caramel mixture. Sprinkle remaining 1/2 cup pecans over batter. Bake 35 to 40 minutes or until edges begin to pull away from sides of pan. Cool completely in pan. Cut into squares. Store in an airtight container.

Yield: about 3 dozen brownies

Dusted with a sweet layer of "snow," our Mini Snowball Snacks pack a chocolate-peanut butter crunch!

MINI SNOWBALL SNACKS

8 cups cocoa-flavored puff cereal
1 package (10 ounces) peanut butter chips
1/2 cup butter or margarine
2 tablespoons light corn syrup
3 cups sifted confectioners sugar

Place cereal in a large bowl. Combine peanut butter chips, butter, and corn syrup in a medium saucepan. Stirring constantly, cook over low heat until chips melt. Pour peanut butter mixture over cereal; stir until evenly coated. Pour about 1 1/2 cups confectioners sugar in each of two 1-gallon resealable plastic bags. Add half of coated cereal to each bag. Gently shake each bag until mixture is evenly coated with sugar. Spread on waxed paper; allow to cool completely. Store in a resealable plastic bag.
Yield: about 10 cups snacks

METRIC EQUIVALENTS

The recipes that appear in this cookbook use the standard United States method for measuring liquid and dry or solid ingredients (teaspoons, tablespoons, and cups). The information on this chart is provided to help cooks outside the U.S. successfully use these recipes. All equivalents are approximate.

METRIC EQUIVALENTS FOR DIFFERENT TYPES OF INGREDIENTS

A standard cup measure of a dry or solid ingredient will vary in weight depending on the type of ingredient. A standard cup of liquid is the same volume for any type of liquid. Use the following chart when converting standard cup measures to grams (weight) or milliliters (volume).

Standard Cup	Fine Powder (ex. flour)	Grain (ex. rice)	Granular (ex. sugar)	Liquid Solids (ex. butter)	Liquid (ex. milk)
1	140 g	150 g	190 g	200 g	240 ml
¾	105 g	113 g	143 g	150 g	180 ml
⅔	93 g	100 g	125 g	133 g	160 ml
½	70 g	75 g	95 g	100 g	120 ml
⅓	47 g	50 g	63 g	67 g	80 ml
¼	35 g	38 g	48 g	50 g	60 ml
⅛	18 g	19 g	24 g	25 g	30 ml

USEFUL EQUIVALENTS FOR LIQUID INGREDIENTS BY VOLUME

¼ tsp						=	1 ml	
½ tsp						=	2 ml	
1 tsp						=	5 ml	
3 tsp	=	1 tbls			=	½ fl oz	=	15 ml
		2 tbls	=	⅛ cup	=	1 fl oz	=	30 ml
		4 tbls	=	¼ cup	=	2 fl oz	=	60 ml
		5⅓ tbls	=	⅓ cup	=	3 fl oz	=	80 ml
		8 tbls	=	½ cup	=	4 fl oz	=	120 ml
		10⅔ tbls	=	⅔ cup	=	5 fl oz	=	160 ml
		12 tbls	=	¾ cup	=	6 fl oz	=	180 ml
		16 tbls	=	1 cup	=	8 fl oz	=	240 ml
		1 pt	=	2 cups	=	16 fl oz	=	480 ml
		1 qt	=	4 cups	=	32 fl oz	=	960 ml
						33 fl oz	=	1000 ml = 1 l

USEFUL EQUIVALENTS FOR DRY INGREDIENTS BY WEIGHT

(To convert ounces to grams, multiply the number of ounces by 30.)

1 oz	=	¹⁄₁₆ lb	=	30 g
4 oz	=	¼ lb	=	120 g
8 oz	=	½ lb	=	240 g
12 oz	=	¾ lb	=	360 g
16 oz	=	1 lb	=	480 g

USEFUL EQUIVALENTS FOR LENGTH

(To convert inches to centimeters, multiply the number of inches by 2.5.)

1 in				=	2.5 cm		
6 in	=	½ ft		=	15 cm		
12 in	=	1 ft		=	30 cm		
36 in	=	3 ft	=	1 yd	=	90 cm	
40 in				=	100 cm	=	1 m

USEFUL EQUIVALENTS FOR COOKING/OVEN TEMPERATURES

	Fahrenheit	Celsius	Gas Mark
Freeze Water	32° F	0° C	
Room Temperature	68° F	20° C	
Boil Water	212° F	100° C	
Bake	325° F	160° C	3
	350° F	180° C	4
	375° F	190° C	5
	400° F	200° C	6
	425° F	220° C	7
	450° F	230° C	8
Broil			Grill

FAVORITE HOLIDAY COOKIES • RECIPE INDEX

ISBN-13: 978-1-60900-025-7